SEAN MICHAEL HANSON

NOVEMBER SHOWERS

Middleton Public Library
7425 Hubbard Avenue
Middleton, WI 53562

SEAN MICHAEL HANSON

NOVEMBER SHOWERS

and Other Poems

North Orchard Press, LLC

NOVEMBER SHOWERS. Copyright © 2021 by Sean Michael Hanson. All rights reserved. Printed in the United States of America. No part of this book may be used or reproduced in any manner whatsoever without written permission except in the case of brief quotations embodied in critical articles and reviews.

This book is a work of fiction. Names, characters, places and events are either products of the author's imagination or are used fictitiously. Any resemblance to actual events or persons, living or dead, is entirely coincidental.

www.northorchardpress.com

ISBN: 978-1-7363148-0-7

for Alex

Contents

Prairie

Dusted Halo - - - - - - 13
Miss Margo - - - - - - 14
The Dream - - - - - - 15
Grim Vibrations - - - - - 17
11-9-2016 - - - - - - 18
Fruit - - - - - - - 19
Skin - - - - - - - 20
This Again - - - - - - 21
The Propulsion Has Died - - - - 23

Thunder

Spite - - - - - - - 27
Influence - - - - - - 28
Tim - - - - - - - 29
At the Bar - - - - - - 30
Hungover - - - - - - 31
Rage - - - - - - - 32
High - - - - - - - 33
awake at night - - - - - 34
Greeting - - - - - - 36
Intangible - - - - - - 37

oot	-	-	-	-	-	-	40
Attn:	-	-	-	-	-	-	41
Gospel	-	-	-	-	-	-	43
Reflections	-	-	-	-	-	-	44
The Patron	-	-	-	-	-	-	46
Vision	-	-	-	-	-	-	47

Seeking November

A Farewell	-	-	-	-	-	-	51
In Praise of Loneliness	-	-	-	-	52
Sore	-	-	-	-	-	-	54
Avert	-	-	-	-	-	-	55
Opposition	-	-	-	-	-	-	56
Blinders	-	-	-	-	-	-	58
11-3-2020	-	-	-	-	-	-	59
Early	-	-	-	-	-	-	60
Stalled	-	-	-	-	-	-	61
Labor	-	-	-	-	-	-	63
No Shower	-	-	-	-	-	-	64
In the Warehouse	-	-	-	-	-	65
Hedging Bets	-	-	-	-	-	-	67
Encounter	-	-	-	-	-	-	69
Revival	-	-	-	-	-	-	70
Post	-	-	-	-	-	-	72
Distance	-	-	-	-	-	-	73
Love Anew	-	-	-	-	-	-	74

Love Reaffirmed	76
Nocturnal Advantage	77
Streetlights	79
Morning	80
GALLAGHER	82
Your Highness	84
Us	85
North	87
Hail Mary	88

Pasture

November Showers	91
Mild Spats	92
At the Dog Park	93
Travis	94
Autumn Heat	96
Proposal	98
Everlasting	100
Dark	102
Acknowledgments	103

Prairie

Dusted Halo

A snow angel flits in my periphery

    sipping whiskey from five-dollar flasks

    and rum cocktails on hardwood floors

    the color of faded honey,

    the color of blonde locks

    washed over by a chocolate river,

    free at last from rooted dam,

    forking around a pearly vista

    blushing gradations of white,

    with a smile like a French press

    that renders my smoky grounds

        into January brew.

Miss Margo

Brown roots creep up to meet the dyed blonde locks,

But I do not pay heed to clashing shades

Because the heart beats on, drums on, and rocks

All thanks to ways in which her hair cascades.

And when the room she enters smiling wide

With questions queued, their answers she must know,

Her warmth laid bare, I only can abide.

You'd swear to God she gleamed from brow to toe.

And though Apollo governs all the day,

He never could the nightly terrors mend.

Not so for Margo am I glad to say.

I never could proclaim a better friend.

And yet I fear her learning thoughts I think,

The somber, crippled thoughts shared with my shrink.

The Dream

The boy is born to a blinding scene

    and progresses never doubting, of course,

        the wolfish dogs that gutted the deer

            sap from pine that sticks like velcro

            peers who scream warmth

            pens scratching lined paper in journals

            theater's thunder

            lightning's roar

            wisps in closets

            faces beneath the bed frame

            moneymen in tailored suits

            sour candies dripping juices

            acid's crawl up the spine

and the knowledge of night's silence.

These and more he never doubts

    yore and yonder.

It never occurs,

    of course.

Grim Vibrations

Rise up, Young Buck, and set to toil.
   Rise up and medicate:
      mouthwash for alcohol, French roast for feeling.
You got jitters, so jolt

awake. Shake off the quakes
   from the murky ink.
Beat back the fog
   and hopscotch from tremor

to tremor. Remember your board
   and ride the not so gentle eddies.
Keep the knees loose lest the moguls,
     those pimply maws,
   gulp you in one jerk.
Flee the seismic minefield
   then set to the sheets
     for deep dreaming,
       deep cover,
     all new aches, and find no difference
between one tide and the next.

11-9-2016

Left up

In the hills with the pine trees

    with the cougars

    and some lonely eagles

I rest

Ejected by the prairie people

Condemned to chew rocks

    and certain rare minerals

Until the next election

Fruit

Strawberry with spines

        Dinosaur accessories

A mutant thing

        Still sweet

Even if hard to swallow

        I'll have another

For I crave

        Good eats

Especially if they tickle

        My stomach lining

Skin

I am the earth, my skin crust,

    body poisoned

Magma pools beneath my face

    and bursts forth through my pores

    marking me scarred with canyons

        their troughs run yellow with pus

        searing and septic

No home remains for purity

    a notion abandoned amidst seismic insecurity

    and frustration pent like a volcano's payload

Wait for the rumble

Listen for thunder

This Again

her ghost left me at the stained table

    as I broke my head upon its wood

        again and again

    growing dull upon the dullest wood

the bone broke

    and shards slit my brain

    quicker than glass

    and spilled my hot anger

        for her

    there upon the wooden table

    to make new stains altogether

now I know

    so long as déjà vu is colored red

lost friends may as well be dead

for death feels much the same

as this same goddamn feeling again

The Propulsion Has Died

Were I to give my dreams breath

       I'd spill them from me like innards

       slashed from my stomach,

       just to give them a little oxygen.

I have the knife.

It's in my hand.

The steel quivers above my twisted navel,

       a procrastinating performer,

       a constipated killer.

The effort is familiar.

The will is foreign.

The Propulsion has died.

Thunder

Spite

My mimicry is malicious

Savage is my intent

Premeditated is my plan

To sow seeds of great dissent

Influence

Dark bidders begin reign at birth
With the first judgment passed

Snakes born of the Original Assumption
Hiss gossip that stains marble

Assumptions written in squid ink
Inject into spines

Words coil around skeletal frames
Puppeteering fragile figures

Bones born white cast black
After the emotional invasion

What remains:
Facsimile of sincerity in flesh

A Shambling Independent
Spreader of Social Contagion

Tim

There once was a cunt named Tim.

My gin, I wouldn't share with him.

For he is insecure and crass,

      an insincere ass

        with an affected laugh,

          bleating like a lonely calf.

At the Bar

Sir, I must insist that you

        do not persist

        lest I be pissed and

        cock my fist and

        maul you like a fucking bear

Hungover

I know not when the ship was sunk

In seas whose names I cannot name.

My memory calls me a drunk

For I, last night, held all the blame.

Rage

I'm angry.

I want to tear someone's eyeballs out with unclipped fingernails.

I want to scream at babies in strollers.

I want to punch everyone I ever loved in the nose.

I want to explode into a swarm of hornets with stingers dipped in liquid hepatitis.

I want to kick helpless animals into a pit of crocodiles.

I want to shank a politician with my car keys.

I want to melt hospitable planets with giant gamma rays.

I want to bludgeon professors with overpriced textbooks.

I want to slit Donald Trump's gizzard with the most savage paper cut in the world.

I want to smash every piece of furniture in this room.

But most of all:

>I want to stop feeling this anger.

High

Bumpy bridges

Rectifying wrongs

Take the tongs and hit the bongs

Play with the Martian monsters

Pretty noses picked by gorgeous little girls singing rhapsodies

Brokers of bristling secrets and hunters of tainted trinkets

Cracking codes

Stacking smokes and taking tokes

Legs tingling at foreign frequencies

Skin rippling like pond water

Bursting at the seams

Chest pulsing with pains

My mind far afield and alit with fire

Let me take another hit

Please

awake at night

yes indeed it is right

yes indeed it is just right
to fight these blights
that steal his breath at night
and in the morning prop a stranger
before the mirror
who looks back with a ruddy mask
made of alcohol and cocoa butter cream
that hides the pits that hold his eyes
and keeps them from sinking further
to the back of his brain before they
crash through bone and back out into the spoiled air
like two drunkards through glass

yes indeed it is a thorough disease
that swaps identities at night and halts
the growth of any one so quick and curt
that the poor boy is whiplashed with a snap
and is made prone by Today who is
jealous of Tomorrow

yes indeed this is an illness grown in a yellowed petri dish
by Today to kill Tomorrow that scrambles
the brain with a morningstar like an egg-beater to yolk
and in the morning the poor boy scarcely knows

what happened

and his thoughts shrivel briefer
but he knows he must fight
to be all right
to not die again before Tomorrow

Greeting

Hello, my friend

      It's been about an age

      since we last spoke

      and we've both grown

      old and leathered

Is that gray in your hair?

      I'll be damned

      I have it too

Intangible

I am a ghost flitting about,
neither harmed nor hindered,
fazed or splintered,
I will suffer no injury.
No swords forged from life's molten metals
will test my mettle with maims or bereavement,
instead passing through my shape,
tasting neither flesh nor bone,
and never boltered with blood.
The harm does not hurt when the heart does not yield.
Look how much easier it is to be
with intangibility as my shield.
I can rest easy when
it all passes through me.

But I forget.

When I am a ghost flitting about,
there is no rest upon supple sheets,
only vigilance at post.
If I'm not scanning surroundings
the sweeter things will pass through,
like the dangers turned trivial,
except the cherished will too.
But even with keen eyes
searching for passersby,
grasping at specters spotted is the only comfort allowed.
I am invincible to both black and white

and I've settled for grey.
And so in my eagerness to escape these binary crowds
it seems I've become a cloud.
A specter in the sky,
a ghost carried by wind.
So far above the world with my destination unknown,
haunting the blue canvas,
riding these waves.

Wait,
was it waves or wind?
I forget.

When everything loved or loathed in the world is
intangible,
then all that remains is my sea of ghosts.
It all passes through me.

It was definitely waves,
if I remember correctly.

How I forget,
how I forget.
How this forgetting turns to
regret.
Even the words I write can't
be kept
in
my
head.
They leak out of my brain like all precious fluids.

I'm intangible, remember?
I can't keep them in there.
 Please don't forget.

But if you'll remember,
there is a way to get rid of this hurt.
Just say the words:

I am a ghost flitting about,
neither harmed nor hindered,
fazed or splintered,
I will suffer no injury.
No swords forged from life's molten metals
will test my mettle with maims or bereavement,
instead passing through my shape,
tasting neither flesh nor bone,
and never boltered with blood.
The harm does not hurt when the heart does not yield.
Look how much easier it is to be
with intangibility as my shield.
I can rest easy when it all passes through me.

oot

Loot scoot root shoot

The aloof doof ruffles through

THE LOOT

Attn:

Classified intel,

need-to-know basis:

>Our blood is gunpowder

>Flesh—plastic explosives

>Every hair a fuse

>>set to ignite every fortnight

>>and tomorrow is the reckoning

>But for today:

>>Keep producing

>>Let not the air's ashy taste

>>>repel your tongue to the

>>>back of your throat

>>>>(Swallowing—Level 2 Hazard)

>>Keep birthing

        words, fluttering distractions

    We need them for the intervals

        between Dark Ages and their

        flashpoints

                (Ignition—Level 5 Hazard)

    Invest in magazines bought at

        grocery store checkout lines

    Follow your daily horoscope and

        complete newspaper puzzles

This is your prescription

        (Diversion—Innocuous)

End of file.

Gospel

It's sometimes better to feel numb in every limb

when you're a True Coward—who prefers

to be a quadriplegic—so that movement, an

overrated sickness, is difficult and villainous.

Movement is Progress and Progress has a fetid

odor at the mouth of Plato's Cave, into which

Brave Fools with fog for ambitions plunge to make

their fog solid.

      Ha!

Who could forsake limbless life when we

Meaty Lumps know quite well the solid stone

beneath our backs? We can see feather for myth, the

sky for dreams. Birds would not neglect Us if they

were real. This is Our Cowardly Gospel.

Reflections

The meat peeks from behind the glass
At turgid dreams in lives long passed

Whirling shadows in familiar shapes
Silhouettes in hallowed mirror landscapes

Gluttonous angels flit beyond sight
Peripheral hints of sallow light

Flirtations flash in glints of fractal selves
Temptations suck eyes—in chasms they delve

The meat seeks a path by way of empath
Back to manifold faces lost to wrath

Upon the meat: geographic history
Stories written in bloody crags and pus seas

Riverbeds and canyons carved in youth
By bubbling acne, acid truth

The meat seeks an ode to its old mission
Reflected in porous pools: a vision

No relic or memorial blister
Only a whisper of a gray whisker

The meat peeks from behind the glass
At turgid dreams in lives long passed.

The Patron

Popcorn kernels lodged in the grooves of my sole—
        —I hate how it crunches under foot—
Air conditioning always too hot or cold—
        —My skin like a film of toasted soot—
Old man staggers in with autumn's breath—
        —"What's the picture this week?"—
"A bloody show about men in the West"—
        —No story for the calm or meek—
"One senior, please, back on the aisle"—
        —"Of course, sir, I know just the seat"—
Rub of the chin, his lips tremble—
        —"Say, I'll also have a treat"—
Wrist flourishes to the sugar trove—
        —"Our selection, sir within the glass case"—
My sticky smile primed to upsell—
        —Paused when a shadow flickers in his face—
"Diane likes chocolate and nougat"—
        —He gestures to Toblerone—
"On a date then, are you, sir?"—
        —"No, my friend, tonight I'm quite alone"—
Candy bought, he shuffles into the theatre—
        —Only patron for the show—
Outside the autumn wind whips on—
        —Whispering of an early season snow—

Vision

get that

grime off

your windshield

no fluid?

no roads

for you

might as

well be

a stone

SEEKING NOVEMBER

A Farewell

Leaving this land with stilted memories,

Washed in emerald pastures and dried

By the willow's browning tendrils drooping

Over the lake yet to freeze.

I think—

      I am contented with whisky dusks

I drink—

Until raptors hail the morn croaking

Love songs, factors of my nightly product—

An unborn romance rolled in papers—

On an ashy, I sit smoking.

Nothing finer than English hellfire!

In Praise of Loneliness

The man, he rises from the tattered couch in the basement
        the olive-green one, with golden seams
just before noon when the sun peeks through the windows
and breathes smoky light onto suspended particles
        pollen and dust
and he wakes with a dammed nose and shuffles upstairs.

The house is empty, his family out
        father working, mother and sister buying groceries
        brought home in brown paper sacks
so he strips, naked and pale, and brews his coffee
        Colombian on the tongue, acidic on the teeth
sipping in chorus to Nirvana on the radio, tapping
a foot on stained linoleum.

He steps through the back door onto a brick patio
        ringed by hostas chewed by rabbits
        and birdhouses hosting twittering lovers
dew wetting his calloused feet, dog hair clinging to soles
from sips to gulps, growing bolder under the peaking sun
        and the proud oaks defying its glare with emerald
        wings to shade the man, their friend, the one
        who never stripped their bark, only as a child, but
        that could be forgiven.

And he thinks to himself:
"It is good that I am alone,
and better that I am not."

Sore

Knees pop every other crack

    in the sidewalk,

lurching forward and backward

    every other step in the unmolded soles

    of these shoes bought on clearance.

Shouldn't have run so doggedly in them,

    breaking them in, or yearning to.

Only breaking my joints.

    Cricking like...crickets.

Laying on a couch with appendages at

    sweet right angles

    breaks (cricks) NOTHING,

    but I'm not sure that's better.

Avert

Nowadays

walking along the cracked sidewalks

everybody keeps their heads down

eyes averted

as if a frail look were enough

to break skin, everybody so sure

that to bleed is to die, that a wound

must be digitized, liked and shared

if it's to be treatable

and never exposed to naked air

lest the wounded fool turn to stone

or some duller substance that cannot accrue

40,000 likes.

Opposition

Shine a light on these grimy times

Starring twisted and mangy mimes

Who parody decent folk

And celebrate unequal yolk.

Croaks the bugle for Light's demise

Its killers we can surmise

To be those red-capped Arians

Who despise all things egalitarian.

So let us rally the disenfranchised:

Neglected bodies humble as Christ,

Who with a plethora of colors will show

This nation is not so white as snow.

Blinders

Humans are marked by

an inability to

visualize scope

11-3-2020

Who's to say where the blindfolded
    Bull roams
Even with the remaining senses intact?
    Sharpened, even.
Who could fire an accurate potshot
At a target nailed to a spinning tree bough
    In a political tornado?

A guy hopes the aimless chaos destroys
    In his favor,
But the guilt derived from selfish mathematics
    Induces a mild
        "Total Subjugation to Fate."

A guy only hopes
Person-to-Person calculus
Produces products congealing
Into Consensus,
Creating outcomes
True to Consensus,
Flush with morality,
Devoid of purple lies.

A guy only hopes.

Early

Brain converted to soup vat

Ingredients such as
    Ibuprofen
    IPAs
    A banana
    A splash of water
    Plain bagel with cream cheese
        (Toasted)

Seasoned with
    3:00AM alarm
    Yowling cat
    Manual labor
    Sweat-soaked mask

Bake for 5 hours at 36°F

Stalled

the lengthy slumber takes

more than it gives.

it seals eyelids with a sticky fog

dunks the brain in molasses

and throttles newborn thoughts.

a good night's rest is earned

piece-meal

with breathless sprints and one eye

aimed at the waking world at all times.

necessary for forward motion—

momentum is a fickle bitch.

so tend to her like you would a

venus fly trap with delicate needs

and never rest while

she's still hungry.

Labor

What is a worker to a boss?

Single-use product

Colored plastic

Destined for the landfill

No Shower

In the rearview mirror

The early morning mashed potato-face

Fluffy with congealed clumps

Uncooked contents in black soup

Dark as inky space

Smoothing out like bread

Under a rolling pin

My lumpy dish

With every mile passed

Hurtling to work with just enough time

To finish the perfect buttered visage

For consumption by labor

In the Warehouse

Laser-prompted beeps permeate every pocket

    Of the bustling cave

Ringing through the webs of all the spiders

    In the steel trusses

The blips are coded—

    "Beep"

        (Select)

    "Beep boop"

        (Sort)

A worker bee loads the package

An offering to the belly

    Hurls back brown dust

Rural-bound trucks rarely cleaned

    Happy faces scribbled in coats by

    Blackened fingers

Every hand a petri dish of collected filth

   From a thousand origins

Grime clings to sweat films homegrown over skin

Brutish breaths from the throat of every

   Harried handler

"Lift with your knees!"

   Cries the strained spine

Muscles struggle to heave parcels streaming

   Down the belt faster than seems reasonable

Takes a true Disciple of Order to succeed

   Even enjoy

   This dogged enterprise

Hedging Bets

I've encountered too

too many

dead-eyed phantoms in the mirror

with all the knowledge of my future

and assurances that I need not worry

about my chances for success because

they say there's a stone tablet somewhere

on top of a mountain

(probably in Greece)

with a big ZERO engraved in its face.

Now I can't say I like their predictions

but what's the point in arguing with

those oily faces when everyone knows

that the slimeballs know failure best

and can spot its acolytes from

an acre away

like certain falcons spy mice in weeds.

Encounter

Your tongue darts to lick my words

      A pink blessing salted by our encounter under

      the weepy light of the slate sky

          In a time for affections prophesied

          by your blue eyes when I strode through

          your threshold

I welcomed it with my own

      A moist return hailing you with GOOD NEWS

      printed in my sweat on your body and yours on mine

          It reads: YOU HAVE ME

          and you better like it

          because I am a happy captive

Revival

No time for
Pyrrhic victories
today—

Only the sweet
scorching womb
of the reborn
phoenix.

Automaton!
Shake off your
rust
and oil thyself.

The fire burns
in thee
again.

Creature in
the shallow sand!
Dart forth and
consume in a
flash of mud.

Hunger no longer.

Yes
I summon thee
to sally forth and
take up the business
of living things
once more.

The Propulsion
has returned.

Post

Nippy winds

nip my nose

their icy feelers blow

hiss goes the snow

dusting the brick walkway

I follow to the post office

waiting for a letter

to show

licked and stamped

written in pen

by you.

Distance

Windblown miles with their cracked black roads

Stretch my heart on an asphalt rack from here to there,

Where you dwell far from me in cities I see in dreams

And dreams and memories of our kisses in dusky dens.

These thoughts are fruits amidst my love-starved labors,

My penny collections, gathered for the day my heart snaps

From this pole, and like rubber slings my soul north

For my costly resettlement within your loving arms.

Until then my heart aches of waiting on the rack

And these meager labors I shall attack while at night

I foresee our future between bookshelves and bars.

My patience has a short wick.

Love Anew

Who could etch into stone

    that two hearts can beat as one?

Not even God is so cocksure,

    the Greatest Doubter of His own absolutes,

        Master of Waylaid Tablets.

Not even He would own the sea serpents

    in Love's uncharted bounds,

        for He is an absentee father

            and an ophidiophobiac.

Fear of Love I learned from Him,

    good son that I am with my purpled

        need to please.

    (She says I have His eyes too,

        dark and furrowed!)

But She insists we paddle onward through

    fog-topped waters—

        maybe land will show.

If only I mentioned, "Before we go—

    I am an aquaphobiac."

Love Reaffirmed

There are mornings for love and mornings for lust;

There is room enough between kisses for honest lies and
      lost trust,

But you and I hold sincere flesh after purple dusks;

Find me in your arms with no want for fuss.

Nocturnal Advantage

Certain objects are better seen under moonlight

    To witness inner qualities most pale

Like the tone of their soul's whisper

    (Does it lilt or purr?)

The echo of their memory

    (Booming or mouselike?)

Or the late night weather they conjure

    (Sleet or fog?)

Identities unseen

Simmer beneath a ghostly sheen

That is only visible

    And only reveals

Traits born of the innermost chasm

When there is no sun to

        Scorch them away

Even without the lunar orb

Darkness can be a better luminary

Than a blinding torch

This is the nocturnal advantage

Streetlights

Lanterns in the night

Clouded windows with sheens of light

Misted by dawn fog

Morning

Your eyes peek at me from beneath heavy lids
When the sun angles its morning mist
Through lazy shutters and shines white on your skin;
A signal I have anticipated, body pressed to yours.

I loose my affections upon you—
Little gremlins, dammed by your slumber, changelings
Taking forms of kisses and curt nibbles—
And you quiver under my palms pasted to your hips.

This was a greeting you expected, and still
You indulge me squeals, pretending you did not know
My dripping intent all through the passage of your dreams,
And that it was twin to yours.

You allow me to press the advantage,
Allow my tongue to subdue yours—pink
And lithe—and for arrogance to seize me before
You drive me back with hidden hordes hungry for love.

They throw me to my back and raise you high to your
    throne
Where you straddle my hips, and I learn I never held sway

So long as your body could be so empowered by Sol's
        warm breath
Pale and sweetened like a sugar I need.

You fasten me to sheets, stained by last night's battle,
With your arms, breasts stroking my face, rallying
Your army of lovesick fires, and whisper, "Good morning."
And so we go to sweaty war and hope it lasts 'til noon.

GALLAGHER

chin rested on the
chair arm

brown eyes bore into my
blue

he wants me to scratch
his head

behind the ears
under the chin
atop the skull

I put down my whiskey to massage
with both hands

he sighs and sniffs like a hog
with a vacuum nose

gives thanks with pleased panting
for taking him in

I give him thanks for padding
into my life

so I scratch under the collar and

call him my Good Boy

my Gallagher

Your Highness

The perfect day is an October flashpoint,

Riding the wind with cheery death and turning leaves,

Gorging the melancholy reservoir,

Raising foaming crests on icy seas,

The land: a floral abattoir,

Humbling spirits whisper in the breeze,

And you—woolen crown upon brow—his acolyte,

    The Autumn King annoints.

Us

I see you on those dusky mornings when your skin is so
pale beneath the weight of light in flight from last
night's snowfall—now blazing white beyond the window.

I see you wrapped in purple sheets, dressed neat—like
always—like an empress in regal hues and lifted shoes
you bought from a Target clearance sale—I'll keep
your secret.

I see your hair in a bun, and your cat, your little son,
swatting it for juvenile fun while I lay on your bed on
my back and chuckle at his probing attack.

I see coffee stains on your shirt when I flirt with you
at work and sip dark roast, waiting for your break when
you'll join me and sate our mutual desire for hungry
love abated.

I see you in my future and past, spurring growth of
wintered grass and flowers which restore my powers of
passion—long frozen of my own admission, to my shame.

I see you, my darling, blue-eyed (sometimes green),
looking back at me through my prickly sheen, stripping

me bare with a glance and bestowing a second chance upon the damned.

I see my redemption in our moments giggling over a whiskey glass, moments when I slap your ass, when you tickle me witless, and when we share kisses between misted windows.

I see you.

I see us.

North

Never seek me

in any land

without pine trees.

Hail Mary

Redemption is a problem for the preternaturally

    Guilty

Freedom from guilt is freedom from purpose

    You wouldn't understand

    It's a Catholic thing

And I haven't been Catholic for a while

So call me

    Intuitively Catholic

Or

    Intuitively Guilty

    as Sin

Pasture

November Showers

Early morning

Soft piano jazz on the radio

I and a few lone travelers

Own the roads

The snow falls thick and warm

Clumps form quick but they are doomed to melt

When the sun rises

So the snow falls fast to make its life count

    Maybe a little out of spite

    But I don't love it any less

When I park I pause

And just sit

And enjoy the trill of the trumpet solo

A perfect moment in this November Shower

Mild Spats

When love is in play,
        Division begets Reconciliation
and I love her anew, just like
our first day together and all
the minutes thereafter.

Each proficient in suturing
        Wounds inflicted upon One Another,
by each other, and our love grows
stronger for it.

We become survivors through
        Surviving the Other,
and become stronger for
the sake of the Other, and for
the sake of Us.

Because love is the worst depressant
and the best stimulant and the only drug
worth the overdose.

Binge love and love binges.

Love drugs drug Love.

At the Dog Park

Tinkling metal tags

Paw prints in dust

Leaves crunch quieter than under any human

    footfall

Travis

An old friend is in town.
He is from Racine, Wisconsin.
I, from Rochester, Minnesota,
now in Minneapolis.
We get beers and swap notes
    on how we've been,
        where we're going.

It's been a year and change.
We are the same age: 23.
In the time apart he has gained:
    a wife
    a child
    a house
    a career.
I have gained:
    an apartment
    a dog
    a long-term relationship
    a few dozen notebooks.
"Hell," we say, "goals have an odd way of living
    and dying."
The beer is cool and brown in the pub's custom
    glass—a local brew.

We're chuckling between sips.

I size him up—new trappings, the same
        young man.
He speaks more, but I'm contented with
        his ideas of creation, so the
        time passes quickly.
It ends. He must return to his family, sleeping
        in the Alumni House. I drive him back.
I park too far from the curb.
        A final chat, a quick goodbye.
I don't see his child—Ben.
        "Maybe next summer," I say.
He walks inside, gone again.

Two hours to make up for a year and change,
        and I think, "Maybe a day will be worth
        a decade."

Autumn Heat

The world is blue in winter on Minnesota mornings. Snow

greets early risers with melancholy stillness painted

on its surface by the moon, and slowly rubbed away by

sunlight. By midday the blankets glitter with newfound

optimism, unaware—or pretending not to care—that

bad follows good and

good follows bad and

bad follows good and

on and on and on

until

the sun lingers longer and the days get hotter, and

before the snow knows it

its glittering glories

die in slush.

Proposal

mountainous pressure
on all sides
betwixt granite molars

building
what physics taught me
      is
potential energy

with seismic force
creeps volcanic undercurrents—
an ultimate zit

in pocket:
the ring

heart chugs like a locomotive—
my angry countdown
      with relentless inertia

…the question…

thank god
she said yes

dormant fires
      sizzle
in a cool bath

to imagine the explosive
      yield
from a no

Everlasting

The secret to sustained love is its regular

and scheduled death and revival

Cyclical rebirth, like the totality of Norse myth

World serpents and horse children included

Because a partnership breeds loveable monstrosities

    Argument artifacts

    Coiled transgressions

    Orange grudges

Because ice miles thick melts slick and runs

    quick under a few focused sun rays

    and carves precious valleys

    —sanctified landscapes—

    with those brutal glaciers

Much like Minnesota topography

settled by Norsemen

Dark

Serpents, serpents, in the trees,

Slither down from turning leaves.

Hissing at the feral wind,

From this season they rescind.

Serpents, serpents, fear the chill!

Void of heat you will turn ill,

Die discarded—hiss your last.

Kiss of winter—year has passed.

Acknowledgements

There are some folks that must be thanked at the conclusion of any creative work's life cycle. This is especially true when the work inspired enough hand-wringing to agitate the moods of everyone in proximity to the creator. My apologies go to all affected by my anxieties as I trekked through this first book, and my special thanks go to the following.

Lydia Smith, for being the best photographer in the greater Twin Cities area, and for assisting me in all things with your boundless energy and creativity.

Devon O'Hara, for reading my manuscript in its fledgling stages, and for validating my work with your kind words.

Mom, for being my emotional bedrock.

Dad, for always pushing me to succeed, and providing unconditional support through every turbulent moment.

Kate, for providing the tough love that all siblings need, as well as being a good friend.

And Alex, for being my love. My passion is sometimes your curse, and I love you all the more for your ability to bear it.

Sean Michael Hanson was born and raised in Rochester, Minnesota. After studying English at Hamline University and working a variety of internships in the publishing field, he founded his own company, North Orchard Press, to put in print the works of aspiring Midwestern authors. He currently lives and writes in the Twin Cities.